Animals Go Home

Patricia Brennan

A Harcourt Achieve Imprint

www.Rigby.com
1-800-531-5015

Fly home, bird.
Where is your home?

Your home is a nest.

Go home, snake.
Where is your home?

Your home is a hole.

Run home, rabbit.
Where is your home?

Your home is a nest.

Go home, spider.
Where is your home?

Your home is a web.

Fly home, bee.
Where is your home?

Your home is a hive.

Hop home, frog.
Where is your home?

Your home is a pond.

Run home, dog.
Where is your home?

Your home is not outside.

Your home is my house!